Hithe

Jennifer Spector

XYLEM BOOKS 2021

Jennifer Spector, *Hithe*

First published in 2021 by Xylem Books

ISBN: 978-1-9163935-4-7

Xylem Books is an imprint of Corbel Stone Press

Hithe

for Clara
through the crossings

&

in memory of my mother, Judith Enrica –'Ricki'–
stone at the waterline

~

if I can't bring home the stars
twine them
as birds do twigs
then perhaps I will wrestle the waves

~

A SAIL HORSE

at Punta San Lorenzo de Veraguas, Panamá

Tell me a story
    Of a thousand birds
        Rousing your children
            Trailed to the ear-slippered earth

Seventy million years ago
Plates diving   divining
    Sea-flood of hawk, buzzard, caracara, tinamou
Weaving possum, deer, fox, armadillo,
    Pirate birds shantying only to rest
On the once-barren hill

Now flushed of life   garnering wind as far
    As Bahía Honda

Geometry hitched to incongruous territories

.

Tell me a story
		Of rain and torches
				Of strident sun riding this green aileron
Of howlers, boas, frogs, deer, the juvenile iguanas
Stricken from clutch   hatching buried nests
Dug to surface   Night-hopping the moon in pods

		Dewlaps displayed
						As they swim through reeds
						A palette of landscape
Swathed in miles   as rove vivarium
With port to San Pedrillo   bleaching longitude

Tracking revenants in this coastal Soná cantata

Of how elements canopy
        Plum rose and ginger, cashew, prestonia,
The corotú parasoled harbour and shade
        & setchell in burrows of grazing
Batten, trumeau, gable   leg and hand
Housed in a wind-shelled pharos

One bird scoring an aria as we collect our tea
    Bristles silver on the soft
Shake of tail   aligns with moon-burned tide

        It is the first morning of time
        And the morning today

SONG FOR THE NIGHTSHADE

a meadow
of seagrass   blue crab
Qi of the whale
land bidding
samphire & aquatic fern
        speedwell   salmon   manatee
foxgloves awaiting bloom

bells straying the prairie
thrum columbine nightshade

echo over the machair
lifting helmet of kelp
& sand   pillowing bent
tussocks   waterforms
oxygen at root

continents tilting the cold

sibylline river courting
the deserted hour
draped in sea-score
& churn of rare flower

shade of sorrel hair whorling
what has brought you here
across the wide arms of the sea?

here, shelter   / here a crest
O breathe the broken letters
how they choke the throat

a spray of order
green of fading song
song fading through body
body passing through the world

what have we
left to suede this
place of shadow?

               old leaning
        without name
making for the old tangles

PARTITIONS

a sketch over tropical land:

rock canyons   *llanos costeros*
olivine burring in displaced cordillera

what if we draw from the edge

                    riving haulage

        bays leashing

                flota de tierra firme

        flags on the map

                    ~

waypoints for schooner
                              foot
                   canoe

            if only brief shapes
          wind-lassed in a trace

of what comes back denuded

                   ~

rasure of sand's landward margins
          & stray ridings

                   ~

all rope for the water   loosened

some by hand

some for tiller

part for the river

FARANDOLE

around this chaparral
finical work is never done;
passerines deck hardworn branch
galvanise soldiers
clouds skit nest to nest
stillwater levies bone

*

from brackish grove
soughing of the season
furnishes a morn
parable of love's vermilion fever

    grass widow
   bird on the harm

MIGRATIONS

blade with me in low
  grasses, stay quiet the pirate
birds and saltarínes deep building rough nests
  spindle the trees

let us lay to ground or
  island for weeks
    to roost on dry cliffs

gliding colibríes, gavilanes, warm updrafts driving
patterns of sea and selvedge
  the Pacific blurring
    the edgelands

dentations hewing
  trough of the body
    something carried in

follow me   sleep near quiet water
trail our carrion at the sound   swimming
          iguanas   headed to islands will walk
     across land
  clutches of thirty
share nests along mangroves and rivers
   even the crocodiles   emerge at night, stalking
swamp brakes

O the waterthrushes sing   few at a time
          over canopies of Malagueto, Jobo, Cecropia
               their mahogany song   a sea-going ship

marked: all the warblers have shored here
     in highlands   in breeding
     dress   they soon depart

& the suicide tree, *Reseco* after a hundred years
     finally matures
   then in April, clusters   brown flowers
    waits for the dry season drops its leaves
 to the wind
  produces dies

not unlike the wanderer
  in snow under way
  & shedding whose every small egress
   first spades   then flights the hollow

A LITTLE WAY

at Los Cayos Holandeses, Guna Yala, Panamá

September's cast
      to the corals   only six ft deep

little fruit has plundered reason
      corners tucked non-geometrically

   come around
      the hatches are opened
the berth is good
      angelfish scatter the keel in
vesture of half-light

   tacking   we watch for wind
      his purled sweep to the bars
where he settles

here for tonight   wooing the white-ruffed manakins
scarlet tanagers and woodcreepers   on slender breach

spelling the course
     we have augury's summer   tying the hawthorns
plump figs and sweet haw and Thalia's port
               ripe cheese lodging in wine

   steady the gooseneck & lane   as sun downs
against a plaza of mangroves

~

who will ask the savannahs
to store their wind
or the asp to orphan leaves?

~

BENTHOS

I

In the first scene she
Is an oneiric wraith
Mother sluiced off the rills
Scaling wavelength of sleep

In the second in flux and swivel
Plumed as the sphynx
Her trancing legato phrases & pitch
Riddle abstrusity

   Somewhere in dying
  What moves in quade falls off
 Cols out to the alders hies from skin
& veering esker gravelled to land

Not the sand scarcely of her
Barchans filling the crescents
Form milled in a locket of sleep

II

The girl lays beside you   on soil
Where her body too   will rue
Wicking the riches
      Sloped days under silt
   Name of her mother   stonebreath
    Blowing pillows of smoke

Talus with thimble
Quelling groundswell
As it courses mottled brim

Heave of life
      Hearth-light
    Rayed to auburn scant
Ash reaching her eyes
In flesh surrender mauving green

She has come to the heart
        Of sight   where dust trace
Of anther and spathe   clovers her body

The praxis to keep on tolling
She knows in the way of love
How it grows wintered with névé

   She will keep walking   to mark faintly
The hone of blood   how it quills a family in
     Breadth   then fledge

It is cold   on the road
        She lets snow into her hand   day is turning
    At the house   a fire is lit

CREPUSCULE

when forest hood is down
pine needles blanket chestnut earth
gold saws raddle in heartwood
grouse flush from the furze

quoins of straw
        fathers   uncles
    brothers of the lake
in rambled pastoral

tents liaised in the maze
yarning lambent runes
to the buttonwoods
damp with brume

delphic phyla
veined off the strawflower
streels cymose florets
from the mottled prow
looking for reasons not to stake

in thicket or say a slink
moon will arrive before them

KINEMATIC

velocity at the valves
of body
a sieve   sound uncrowded
like a moon probe

obey the audition
tune with new ear
vane of roof
crosshatching

the physical versus
the signal

they speak of the horn in the hunt
a soundmark
sure, the wolfbeat again

original sonic event

        leads to a pinwheel—

    it starts with sky
   moves inward
the fore impulse

 come, stage right:
   dæmon
        /jester
   tempus stows breves
cranes toward the strand

swarms the object
    absorbing washes

     & with paddle and aulos
alterity glides the interval
  in her willow coracle
     dwellen
dishevelled like all ancient things

a shepherdess
at the floodway   ear to the sheepbells
gauging the state of her flock

yes   she hears music
trilling the skerry

welling the ear
harmonic pitching
node lashes   of seiche
or birch through embrasure

& in   thatching the roundhouse

TRILOGY

at Jaramillo Arriba, Chiriquí, Panamá

I. The Bull

we find in morning beam
amid pine & oak bending
with wind   a spectral visitor
          near inhabitant
  waiving buff territory

light spears the path
limns bull & bosk   vaulting
          aureole before midnight's wolf
                moon slings her charcoal hood
                over sloughing sun

a scuttle of silhouettes
    against the brindled mountain
        fringing the selvedge

the bull rises
takes his dust-cut steps
in shamble as we pass

long after leaving
his golden fescue
    invisible   indivisible *being*
like thunder from the corpse

      fracture a day
   & it holds part of you

2. Hillside

I

Volcán Barú bedding down
near indirect eruption
tuff cones & loam depth marks
   impact sites   wind currents
                       plied extremes
a shelling cant of residue

hybrid human-animal remains
      & admixed carpi
in states of crumbling alliance

II

not far from the village
Ngäbe girls in traditional dress
hold time in nacarat, heliotrope, emerald *naguas*
catch spires of straw heat
off the shelf   streaming the *bajareque*

    & water-borne guardians
rounding shifts travel as message
new wood   trace ceramic vessels   maps sketched
into stone   bone offerings at the hem
                          of the grave

sandbox tree once held sand for ink
    also shaped *cayucos*, cattle fences
   & huntsman's poisoned arrows
the miniature body smashing crude
        objects
    tapir or honeybee
   hives in the river rush
                                                                                       serranía

in a chain of connection

III

telluric synergies
     of last things

crops   old-growth forest
petroglyph sites   shamanistic reassembly
   nest of the Quetzal

rifted
above ground
schemata—

charted passage:
flutes from the femur   feathers
textiles   skin of jaguar & stones
  the hold of body timber

IV

aeolian lifts   not far from the oak
carry scat & tracks from the hide

  place unearthed
    & drifting
currach of body trawling
rode   swelling
    natal distance

V

       & the rough house
    in mid-step moving
roots   grass & river
grafts what carried from
kyle & baleen to humic stratum

anchored by slim freight
sward still billeting green

3. Archer

first or second burial
soil stains unclear
as indicated by earth

a frottage of the body
disclaiming hull &
waterline by the hollows

ground-cloth and lacustrine
blades in a strike of shieling
small molds cupping The Three Graces

fletching the wind with summer's arrow
sienna pine scatters the floor
the *bajareque* peaks the mountain

mobility / sign / figure & landscape
interplay of relinquishing outlines

almost an outcry –
    January's unspent cloud
    trained on the mountain

RIVERBRIDGE

I

an outwork of wind
Notos' hazed assemblage
crowding all sail

    mother
      squall   fox sparrows'
        few spruce nests   fled in gales

pine barrens & drift foundation
reeving sand & seaoats in
plait of disembarkment

swift reeled with awn
& skeins from wooded
spar with body truss

she   a winter chord
          whelming her shelter

     bridging floe & water towers

II

       that much water
       large of miles
       let the body go

all her stone could speak be told
      & breath for bluff indents
         cooling in their green

     to say you were a *dwelling*
       and *I* a bridge   strand daughter

SAND HWYL

I

sea loosed of timbre   fallows breaching
   a sable dim-wood sky
       greydune   pitch   the outswelled iris
             brome grasses left
       & the field-brain mazing with mallow
            in fetch of wind thraw

   & the beak-bitten roses   twitched of source
     whose sutured crowns tipping gambits
  in harn of the thirstland

make an overture:
sandwings ally to bow   freight the slue
   abandon the bank for breadth of the salt-scowed body
     taken by rims   plumbing long-marks in the pirr

II

bitterns and fulmars booming
       through the haugh
            wick their wings on juddered thills
          & have scried how
             hyaline seam
          will sail its bodyflower

& how pocked bricks testify to the toil of bees
     a symphonic gather of
          mass & greenwood

              a charge of direction in maritime space
the sea arch in cliff & shale wends
    canorous unearthings from water scarred hushes
        to hymning water-carved bridge

hachures shunt in loom of skin

III

windward marks:

1. a haunt of treading over yellow sedge
2. foreland winnowing hurst
3. limbs from brumal sheets
4. ash thwarts abandoned
5. water trenched in tilth

a narrative scatter
landing

sea-thrift   & mouthprints
breath of the night rower

attar of the emptied body
under vital wreck
turning rose cloth
& timber
to the crossing forms

~

know
the cold
how it rips your skirt
dances the grave
shuttles its many nests

this breath
did you suspect
flush scooped
of own dark weep?

~

INVITATION

Run to earth
Ground is singing
Eidolon tuned by door
Terremoto terrane cleaving
Land extruded from mountain

Down by the rock pool *collision*
Pillow lava marled to the gape
Relict of seamount   crest of fount
Paean to massive migration

Tumble down
Let us skim this cave
Rail precipice   dance on the berm
Bird and wave
The blonde arcade skippering our boat

I'll sing the blues of a limning earth
Lodestar flint and lantern
Lea festooned with riband parades
Signaling mutation

Run to earth
Ground is broken
Bedding trim of stitch

Headlands crumple like almond seifs
There is stone where needed

CROQUIS

in an absolute visual
          energy pool
natural chaos

          we make these things:

                    sage brushes
                    soil drumlins
                              first maps
               graves that rivered

                    The reined backwater
                                   animals traverse
     tow and plashing in
          furrowing
               breaklines

beside lake palms
& fields
some with their fishing rods
                             hawsers streeling

                    The shorn covert clearing loess
                             scree   charcoal

                    a modello for canvas
                                   ravelled by wind

sanguine flags
                    tones   from broken tors
          a gesture   of the carry of clouds
                             the skub-lided bestiary

                                        below the clints

& places of shipwreck dashed by roseate
      stencil   histories tinned

        the marram bowing shivered brae

   lotic sediment
   hand-drawn topography lines
      the fin of roots
   thawl, wingspan, fell

7, 2012

reassess
        ability to clearly communicate
                internal consciousness

abundant becoming calls
        for reevaluation of field-brain circuits
                perception disrupted fact
                        non-survey correlates

                substrates not confined aroused
                        humans critically
        regions
    feeling states
instinctual punishing systems
where young human mind supporting
        decision appear

                    arisen as evident
birds in parallel consciousness near
grey microcircuitries   found patterns of sleep

            as in zebra finches to magpies striking
humans, great apes, dolphins and elephants
                  in self-recognition
                      disruption

feedback interventions
            non-human compounds affect
                    lead to awareness which evidence
                      emotional networks

          evolutionary absence does not preclude
experiencing non-human animals
             with capacity

                        to weight consciousness

                        and presence

BAVARDAGE

      here there were trees
    here grass

    you might say
  catastrophe of matter

datum of the quiet perishing earth
      passing dispatches

property   a road   plein air tension

    & boundaries of siphoned ground

these were the riches
flaring whalebone darts

intel wrangled
bodies off the scarp

      & kettledrums in the field
where bison once flooded the river

THREE TRACTS IN THE WELKIN

I   Shaw

a sun goddess who hid
       from the sun

who chose her sword
         wood away
             & galloped with oars flycut to the wind

trailing her hawks
the swimming iris wold
combing àirde & mountain heather
throne-floating divine waters
               & daughters shifting

into wives
       pictographs
       apologues

she with her lion
          finger in jaw
       seat to the rising sun

vis divina   vis humana   vis naturalis

II   Cirque

Ra rides the solar barque
                querls the trim-necked evening

                            greyfelt
                                on a broken strain
                                    muttering of the old kingdom
            when swallowed   Ra cords the sun
& returns in the kiln of morning
chooses his sword
            energies brune

            & daughters were borne unto them they'll sing
                    plumped from the craven hours
                        mothers worth more than their wide berth

& the falcons
        clearing shards from the ruined city
                eyrie mute
        fastening their talons

III   Varve

land unsifted
unlike her body travelled through by night
summer and winter
a sky goddess
    sleighing the marches
                rends to savage lioness
      her sway of track   lacing thaw

              rathe & sighted
                      in open waiver

MID-RUTTIER

I

Naenia slaked by flame
late-breath in maw
  of winter   snowfern
  & reedbeds   fray off mother
rick and tinder

December's grained watchings
casting jettons on the slab
an abacus drawing dust through the
prescient rowans   & crossed points
in ruttier & desertum

       is it work of the sea
   what crowds a room?

if I were glove if I were spiral if I swale if I
were angle of firespeak if I castle if I were drawer
if I three stones to air if tattle I if fail if I terraria
chose or stair if ocelot if newly rare if I
foreigner if tracking mere if I fetch were if I where
and were I home

II

where to hunt
      where to crawl
what intoning from plum interior?

aural loads   cold fleet
traction braiding
what travelled before us
to the living shed of earth
   & language in temporal mechanisms

strath of body
     boat and drifter
   pulling material copresence

for every photon   Earth
giving her twenty more
salt ringing broad basins
autumn's quitch & sere fruit
wreathed in emergence

hithe of discards
tipped of *place*
briefly landing
extension

III

at the tide-gate
half-timbered
banked canoes and
waders   rimming sand
unsaying low water

> *if I timber if I decay if young if crudely made*
> *if I present tide unworn if ream if pond if I core*
> *if I were linnets or if stone-rivered if I grow*
> *wood if I were giver if motion stolen if I*
> *were buttoned if I were bole if I ilex or*
> *foal were I or if another this place I thriftflower*

is house the girl?
structural bow under gauged reliction

returned   flyping the thatch
cordage   rift limb
ground-patter in new distance

IV

what last bodice
diminished structure
dissembled in the straits
draws larch across lound quay?

    to the boathouse
    waymarked in the ruins
  running for the river

wood if given   if motion rendered
if I were reume if swift frostbarrow if silk if sled if I
cower if odic lent were I nightwaiver if I kedge to
cindered hour off salt or forward saddle if I shed
or burn chart-echo if shore if terns if I marrow
tacent transfer

    pinning the groundsel
        to fret measure

THE ARROW

Now   the winds
sail disquiet
      scour the fields
        for that heart in port

      who is sounding at the breaks
      slippering dark rooms
    what shards and glyphs chisel
      camber in the heart?

where I have landed
    there is bark to be carried
        and plinths to root

      blistered with scorch
        the wrack flower

       it is the hour   we who have wildered
     burn our cressets
       turn back to the road
   outskirt the village
try our broken drums

something
       luffed in the wind
caught like bloom &

     must on the whaled skiff
    where I am laid

ferries me

    say the dryland arrows
   also are turning

AUTUMN

                    unfurls her
               orange leaves
            her grey morning

        & that premonition
                    we call winter

        revisits every tree

        *

                         however brief
                                        return
        changed by the route took

NOTIONS LEFT

winter sails the branches
  follows the deer
    passes the wormwood

        passes the drifter   also following
  the snow
a kind of charter

 or perhaps notion
  that our leaving is marked

AFIELD

what wreckage

    combed in tethered broach
        shores the spheric house

tideway slaked with beeches
buck & beam assailed by sough
        swifts darting the frame

    as far from surface as from float
sewed where water ground her

        shoaled of breath
      shorn of wind

      dishabited
        barest shelter

swash & wild clover   ransomed
by what coves the shed

        & like the rose
    tied to stone which wends
the brick which bees have holed

little thorns & white flower
presage the coming summer

        it will be enough for thrift
    to grow where sound has been

GLOSSARY

Abacus	sand or dust table used for arithmetic calculations and drawings with placed pebbles or tokens.
Aileron	the moving wing of an airplane.
Àirde	GAELIC; a place of elevation and high altitude.
Aulos	double-reeded wind instrument from Ancient Greece.
Bajareque	SPANISH (usage in Panama); the drizzle of high mountainous regions sometimes accompanied by light mist and fog.
Barchans	sand dunes shaped and sloped on the windward side gradually shifting by the erosion of sand and wind.
Bosk	a grove of thickets and underwood.

Brae   SCOTS; the steep brow or side of a hill.

Cayucos   SPANISH; wood-hewn canoes dug from
                  a singular tree trunk.

Cirque   a concave, steep-sided corrie resulting
                  from glacial erosion.

Colibríes   SPANISH; hummingbirds.

Cordillera   a continuous, complex mountain
                  range.

Corotú   SPANISH; a tropical, flowering tree
                  native to Panama, *Enterolobium
                  cyclocarpum*, known in English as
                  elephant-ear tree.

Cressets   lights or beacons in the form of metal
                  baskets set on poles filled with ignited
                  wood or coal.

Dæmon   (LATIN spelling); an unseen spirit
                  guide between the mortal and divine,
                  of dual nature, presiding over each
                  person from birth, figuring in Greek
                  mythology.

Desertum	LATIN; a barren place of the wild.
Dim-wood	a sky without visible stars.
Dwellen	MIDDLE ENGLISH; to remain, to reside.
Eidolon	an ideal or idealised place, person or thing; a spectral force of nature.
Embrasure	a wall aperture that enlarges the interior outline for a window or door.
Esker	a ridge of glacial gravel, sand and sediment deposits.
Fetch	the span of unobstructed wind-travel across water, which upon reaching shore may contribute to flooding and longshore drift.
Gavilanes	SPANISH; sparrowhawks.
Hachures	lines used in maps for the shading of hills and the steepness of slope inclines.

Hithe from the OLD ENGLISH; a landing by a river, or the shore where boats may rest to disembark or load.

Hurst a shoal in the sea.

Hushes scars left in the landscape after rushing waterflow separates stone and earth from the washed surface.

Hwyl from the WELSH; the sail of a ship; in the older sense of the word, a course taken at sea.

Jettons coin medals or tokens used for calculations on an abacus or counting board.

Jobo SPANISH; the *Spondias mombin*, native tree to the tropical Americas whose fruit is used for many confections and whose leaves possess medicinal properties.

Llanos costeros SPANISH; low coastal plains formed by falling ocean levels, extending inland.

Lound   NAUTICAL; out of the wind's path;
           tranquil.

Machair   SCOTS; an expanse of low grazing land
             near the sea covered with grasses or
             sometimes wildflowers.

Malagueto   SPANISH; the *Xylopia frutescens* tree,
               native to the tropical Americas, of the
               Annonaceae family.

Nacarat   a vivid shade of light red-orange.

Naenia   Roman goddess associated with funer-
            ary grieving and a person's death.

Naguas   ankle-length, short-sleeved dresses
            worn by the Ngäbe women in Panama.
            The sewn geometric patterns adorn-
            ing neckline, skirt hem and waist are
            referred to as 'dientes' (teeth), and
            represent the river current, the teeth of
            animals and mountain peaks.

Ngäbe　　　　one of the seven surviving isthmian
　　　　　　Indigenous peoples of Panama whose
　　　　　　comarca (territorial land) encom-
　　　　　　passes regions within three adjacent
　　　　　　Northwestern provinces, those of
　　　　　　Chiriquí, Bocas del Toro and Veraguas.

Notus　　　　Greek god of the south wind; one of
　　　　　　the four *Anemoi* (wind gods), known
　　　　　　in Roman mythology as Auster, whose
　　　　　　storms and threatening winds of
　　　　　　autumn and late summer were feared.

Pharos　　　　from the GREEK; a lighthouse.

Pitch　　　　NAUTICAL; the sway of a ship and its
　　　　　　motion under strain from bow to stern.

Quade　　　　unsteady and changeable.

Quitch　　　　fast-growing, coarse grass which can
　　　　　　overtake an area.

Ra　　　　supreme Egyptian sun god revered for
　　　　　　possessing the power of life, creation of
　　　　　　earth and its seasons, plants, animals,
　　　　　　heaven and the underworld.

Rathe   arriving with speed and promptness;
                   coming in early.

Reume   NAUTICAL; an old term for the tide.

Ruttier   a sailing logbook of the sea in usage
                   prior to the development of charts,
                   containing navigational and geograph-
                   ical information, notes on winds and
                   tides, trade routes, ports and other
                   relevant directions.

Saltarines   SPANISH; manakin birds.

Sandwings   the 'wings' that form around a boat
                   discarded in the sand.

Seiche   an oscillating standing wave in a body
                   of water, coastal inlets, lakes or seas
                   caused by wind and variations in baro-
                   metric pressure.

Serranía   SPANISH; a chain of lower-lying
                   mountain ranges which form part of a
                   cordillera.

Sewed NAUTICAL; (of a ship) resting where water has lowered, unable to float until the return tide.

Shaw SCOTS; a wood of natural growth consisting of small trees.

Skub SCOTS; a light passing rain and mist.

Tacent unspoken.

Terrane crustal rock formation that through tectonic processes has been transported.

Terremoto SPANISH; earthquake.

Thalia the eighth of the nine Greek mythological muses, associated with poetry, joy and comedy.

Thawl a hole in stone walls that allows for the passage of livestock.

Thraw SCOTS; a twisted, curving turn.

Three Graces   Greek mythological goddesses of hap-
                  piness, beauty, creativity, charm and
                  play, known as the Charites.

Thwarts   crosswise seats in a boat for a rower.

ACKNOWLEDGEMENTS

The work assembled here has passed through many routes and taken various forms. Many people and places have accompanied me, more than I may mention, but to each of you I offer my gratitude for the unique ways in which I have felt encouraged.

Many thanks to Richard Skelton & Autumn Richardson, the publishers and editors of Corbel Stone Press and Xylem Books, for the continuing interest over the years, which has led to *Hithe*. The singular editorial and aesthetic vision woven through all your publications is inspiring, and I am grateful to have found stitch in these folds.

To Martine Bellen, whose discerning, fine eye and ear helped shape and guide these poems over fluctuating tides; to you I send a flare of thanks.

Thank you to the editors of the journals, chapbooks, and artists' books in which many of these poems first appeared:

Reliquiae, Shearsman, Alterity, Litmus Magazine, Molly Bloom, La Vague, Nature & Sentience (Contemporary Poetry

Series), Rebecca Clark's *Book of Hours, Suelo* (Estudio Nuboso), *& Tzak*.

The poem 7, 2012 was commissioned by the Centre for Alterity Studies and was composed as an erasure from *The Cambridge Declaration on Consciousness*.

Many thanks to family, friends & collaborators in no particular order, with whom I have been aligned, sharing creative spaces generously opened; Alan Spector, the late Carl Marzani, Charlotte Pomerantz, Gabrielle Rose Marzani, Tony Marzani & G. Harry Schroder, Jason Cutler, Max & Alyia Cutler, Tamar M. Spector Pikler, David & Esther Spector, all my Icaza family, and to Gabriel Icaza & Lezlie Milson pine-bundled thanks for the Boquete writing sojourns. For the entwining; Valérie Ancelle Leblet & Yves Leblet of Artlodge Panama, Hoa Nguyen, Valerie Hird, Vanessa Kamp, Vivian Heller, Rebecca Clark, Liza Z. Kovacs, Robert Ajar, Laura Watt & Clark Thompson, Shira & Marnie Berk, James Hood & Heather Andrews & S/V Charmer, Karen Holmberg for her absorbing research at Volcán Barú in Chiriquí, Panama, Ela Spalding, Claire Pentecost & Brian Holmes. At every turn, a sweep of thanks to Clara Icaza for the incisive reading of this work. In memoriam for their early support, thanks to the late Alvin Feinman, and the late Jane Connor Marcus.

CPSIA information can be obtained
at www.ICGtesting.com
Printed in the USA
BVHW042333160521
607527BV00014B/681